MORE THAN THE LOVE OF WISDOM

An Introduction to the Whole of Philosophy

David Jensen
Brigham Young University

cognella
San Diego, CA

Bassim Hamadeh, CEO and Publisher
Christopher Foster, General Vice President
Michael Simpson, Vice President of Acquisitions
Jessica Knott, Managing Editor
Kevin Fahey, Marketing Manager
Jess Busch, Senior Graphic Designer

First published in the United States of America in 2013 by Cognella, Inc.

Trademark Notice: Product or corporate names may be trademarks or registered trademarks, and are used only for identification and explanation without intent to infringe.

File licensed by www.depositphotos.com/

Printed in the United States of America

ISBN: 978-1-62131-099-0

www.cognella.com 800.200.3908

Acknowledgments

I wish to thank my many students over the past 12 years for whom the content of this book began as a series of lectures. I wanted to address the problem of how to straightforwardly and informatively answer the question "what is philosophy." Although this may be thought of as a question for introductory students, in fact I first engaged my advanced students, philosophy majors, with the discussion. My hope was to provide an answer that would unify the diverse topics they had studied as majors. Their thoughtful questions and feedback have been invaluable to bringing this discussion to its present state.

My student and research assistant Jandon Mitchell deserves special mention. In the Summer of 2007 he helped me to prepare the first written draft of this work. Jandon has an eye for good form and an ability to "share a vision." Having heard the lectures on several occasions, he helped me bring the attitude and tone of the lectures to the written form.

I am also grateful to the team at Cognella, and my editor Jessica Knott, for encouraging the novel approach I am attempting in this book. I am surrounded by excellent colleagues and teachers at the Philosophy department at Brigham Young University who have mentored me both as a student and a teacher. As always, my family, and especially my wife Ashley, have been a bedrock of support in the ups and downs of my young career in academia.

A few years ago my then 5 year old son Daniel asked me out of the blue, from the backseat of the car, "what is philosophy?" He knew enough to know I was a teacher, and my subject was philosophy; I could tell he had been thinking about it. I tried to evade the question by answering "it's what Dad teaches." He immediately detected my fraud and replied "I know, but what is it?" This book is dedicated to him and to answering that question.

Contents

Chapter One

Philosophy Is Not *the Love of Wisdom*

P hilosophy is the most enduring, evolving, and prolific discipline in the Western intellectual tradition. Despite its importance, the discipline of philosophy itself is poorly understood outside of the philosophical community. The goal of this book will be to develop for those new to philosophy a correct and informative characterization of what philosophy is. We will focus less on the details of particular philosophical issues and past philosophers and instead understand philosophy as a whole. Many introductory philosophy books begin by only briefly describing the whole of philosophy before delving into a discussion of philosophical questions and problems or historical figures and writings. We depart from this approach in at least two important ways. First, we begin negatively, in this chapter, by criticizing several popular but incorrect characterizations of philosophy. Students who adhere to these misguided conceptions of philosophy often have a difficult time moving past them. Thus, some direct discussion of them is in order. Second, we will not discuss the best characterization of philosophy until the fourth and last chapter. Starting in Chapter Two (and continuing through Chapter Four), we will work positively toward understanding what philosophy is through a discussion of the question itself, the issues that philosophers discuss, the history of philosophy, and its role in our larger intellectual tradition. Given the difficulty of understanding what philosophy is—indeed it is a challenging undertaking—this process of working toward an answer will promote a more nuanced, meaningful, and enduring understanding of philosophy in contrast to merely "being told" what it is. This detailed understanding will provide you with a broad foundation for more in-depth studies of philosophical writings, topics, and problems.

Popular Misconceptions

As a student and teacher of philosophy, I've heard dozens of incomplete or incorrect answers to the question of what philosophy is. We'll consider some of these answers in this chapter, none of which are unreasonable, and in fact, they each contain a kernel of truth. As it turns out, most of these answers originate from looking at some nonessential part or aspect of philosophy and drawing from it a conclusion about the whole of philosophy. We will consider the following misconceptions, which characterize philosophy as

1. Thought-provoking stories and interesting intellectual anecdotes.
2. Words of wisdom with hidden contradictions; the search for paradoxical conclusions.
3. "Deep thinking," pondering, or discussing important topics
4. The study of the unanswerable or unprovable.
5. Secularized religion.
6. The love of wisdom.

(1) Thought-provoking stories and interesting intellectual anecdotes

Philosophy does indeed involve peculiar and interesting anecdotes and stories. A classic example is the myth of Gyge's ring in Plato's *Republic*. In conversation with Socrates, Glaucon tells a story about a shepherd who finds a magical ring that makes its wearer invisible, thus enabling its wearer to do anything he or she wants with impunity. Upon discovering this power, what does the shepherd use his newfound ring to do? He becomes a servant of the king, seduces the queen, and with the aid of the ring kills the king and takes possession of the kingdom! Glaucon tells this story in order to draw attention to a question about morally right and wrong behavior, namely, what reason would the wearer of the ring have for not engaging in immoral behavior that would be to his or her benefit (*Republic* 359–360)?

In the case of the shepherd, why not use the ring to kill the king and take possession of his kingdom.

Though these sorts of stories are used in philosophical discussion, they are not the essence of philosophy. First, only some philosophers use stories or anecdotes of this sort. Second, when they are used, they are used to illustrate a larger philosophical issue or question. In the story of Gyge's ring, the issue is whether there is something inherently wrong with so-called morally wrong behavior, or if the wrongness of morally wrong behavior merely stems from the fact that we might get caught and be punished. So these stories function to illustrate a question, to demonstrate a problem, and at times to argue for a conclusion. In this respect they are important to doing philosophy, but they do not characterize philosophy as a whole.

In addition, many thought-provoking stories or anecdotes are not philosophical. A famous story of King Solomon in the Bible involves two women who each claim that a baby is hers and come to Solomon to resolve the matter (1 Kings 3). Solomon's resolution is to cut the baby in two and give half to each woman. One woman immediately pleads with Solomon not to divide, and consequently kill, the child but to give the child to the other woman. Solomon concludes that this woman was in fact the mother of the child because, he reasons, the actual mother would prefer the child at least live, even if not in her keeping. He then gives the child to her. Is this an interesting and thought-provoking story? Certainly. Philosophical? Not really. It may tell us something about the wisdom of Solomon, and probably something about human psychology, but it does not have philosophical content.

(2) Words of wisdom with hidden contradictions; the search for paradoxical conclusions

You may have heard the statement that "the best defense is a good offense." This phrase has a certain appeal because it sounds both true and self-contradictory. If offense is the opposite of defense, then how can the best defense be an offense? Statements like this have a powerful rhetorical effect, as if the contradictory appearance of the statement signifies that some profound truth has been revealed. The claim is of course really not so puzzling: sometimes the best way to defend oneself is to go on the attack rather than wait to be attacked. Whether such contradictions (some can be termed "oxymorons") really are puzzling, or contain words of wisdom, or reveal profound truths, however, has nothing to do with philosophy.

Some of the confusion here stems from the fact that philosophy does deal with paradoxical statements and situations. Here's an instance of a familiar paradox called the "liar's paradox." Suppose John always lies. If John says to you, "I always lie," then is what he says true or false? Since he always lies, then it seems as if what he says—"I always lie"—is true. But then he will have said something true, and we have already stated that he always lies. But if what he says is not true, and given that he said "I always lie," then it follows that he does not always lie. But, again, we have already assumed that he always lies. So we are in a predicament because what he says appears incapable of being either true or false: we have a paradoxical situation. Do philosophers deal with paradoxical situations like this? Yes.[1] However, as with the example of the myth of Gyge's ring, these paradoxes occur in only some philosophy, and they usually serve a larger purpose.

Furthermore, the resolution of a paradox is not necessarily the aim of philosophical inquiry. For example, one ethical paradox is called the paradox of happiness: the harder you try to be happy, the less likely you are to be happy. This seems to express a genuine truth about happiness. If a person puts forth too much deliberate effort to be happy—is continually focused on it and acts with it as an explicit goal—then he or she is less likely to find happiness. And yet the claim is paradoxical; for, we think of happiness as the goal of life and so it should follow that putting forth more effort for the sake of happiness would lead to happiness. As it stands, this paradox seems to express a fact about life and happiness. Thus, the point of the ethical philosopher is not to "solve" or "explain away" this paradox but to make sure it is accounted for in their theorizing.

Finally we note that, as with the case of interesting intellectual anecdotes, not all paradoxes are philosophical. A good example is the apparent paradox we started with: "the best defense is a good offense." These kinds of statements often express truths, typically in a memorable way, but their philosophical relevance, if any, is another matter.

---

1   For example, a famous paper by Alfred Tarski (1901–1983), "The Semantic Conception of Truth" takes seriously the liar's paradox as a problem that a systematic treatment of truth must avoid.

(3) "Deep thinking," pondering, or discussing important topics

In English we use the term "philosophy" and "philosophical" in ways that are not related to the discipline of philosophy that is studied at universities and that has a history going back to the ancient Greeks. People say, for example, "My philosophy is that you should never acquire credit card debt," or "My philosophy of customer service is that the customer is always right." When the term "philosophy" is used in these contexts, it is not referring to the same thing we are trying to articulate in this book. It is a generic term for "view" or "theory." It is perfectly correct to use the word "philosophy" in these senses but it is not the use of the word "philosophy" that we are talking about, and you should always keep in mind this difference. Thus, people who discourse on this and that matter—"My philosophy of ... is," "My view about ... is that"—are not necessarily doing philosophy or being philosophers. Philosophy is a discipline that has specific topics and questions; it is not merely a thoughtful or opinionated way of approaching any topic.

Further, I sometimes hear students talk of philosophy as "deep thinking." This understanding of philosophy is best avoided. While it may be true that lots of philosophy involves "deep thinking"—this probably means thinking about things that are difficult to think about, thinking rigorously, systematically, and with diligence—there is plenty of deep thinking that is not philosophical. Someone who thinks deeply about the structure of the atom is not doing philosophy, but is doing physics. Someone who thinks deeply and seriously about political elections is engaging in political science. Deep thinking and discussion occur in all sorts of inquiries and with all sorts of topics that are not philosophical. So while "deep thinking" may describe philosophical inquiry, it describes many other sorts of inquiry as well.

The view of philosophy as "deep thinking" may stem partly from some of the claims or questions that philosophers ask. For example, the early Greek philosopher Heraclitus (c. 540–480 BC) is famous for having said "you cannot step in the same river twice." Does this sound deep? Perhaps. In fact, some, when hearing such claims, are turned off to philosophy: surely one can step in the same river twice, and any discipline that makes claims to the contrary must be pointless! In fact, neither view is right. Heraclitus is simply drawing attention to a puzzle about how we think and talk about physical objects. We think of a physical object as a continuous piece of matter with well-defined borders. But when it comes to something like a river, we encounter a problem. On the one hand, we think of a river as a physical object, and we talk about it as if it is persistent. A person can live by the Mississippi, point to it, cross over it, touch it, and so forth. On the other hand, we know that the physical composition of a river, the water, is constantly changing. In fact, over a period of time, all the water in the Mississippi will have flowed out to sea and new water will take its place, hence you "can't" step in it twice. So there is a puzzle to be solved about what kind of an object a river is, how the Mississippi can be the Mississippi even though its composition is continually changing. The question is reasonable. Whether it is a "deep question" or "deep thinking" is another matter and may depend on the purpose in posing the question.

This mistaken view of philosophy as "deep thinking" reveals something important about our attempt to answer the question *what is philosophy*. We want our answer to distinguish philosophy from other disciplines. Because an answer like "deep thinking" also describes chemistry, biology, physics, psychology, and so forth, it fails to distinguish philosophy. Distinction from other disciplines is not the only criterion for a correct answer, but it is essential and its importance should be kept in mind as we attempt to characterize philosophy.

(4) The study of the unanswerable or unprovable

Some mistakenly believe that philosophy is the study of unanswerable questions or unprovable answers, questions for which there may be a correct answer but which we could never prove. We will return to this later in the book (toward the end of Chapter Three) when we have developed a better understanding of the history of philosophy. The quick response to this conception of philosophy is simple: no philosopher thinks of himself or herself as "answering" unanswerable questions. We do not think: *here are some questions I do not believe can be answered, but I'm going to study them and seek answers nevertheless*. That would surely be an odd undertaking.

There are several concerns with the notion of *answering a question* that is assumed by this characterization of philosophy. For one thing, answers to some questions come in parts. Consider the question: how does the human heart function? This question has been answered (and continues to be answered) over the course of centuries. For example, it wasn't until 1628 that William Harvey discovered the correct manner in which circulation occurs (arteries send blood out to the body parts, veins return it for re-oxygenation). That was a *part* of the answer to the question of how the human heart functions. Presently, we have a better (more complete) answer to the question of how the human heart functions. Decades from now, we can suppose that the answer will be yet improved. The same holds true with philosophical questions. Many are answered in parts, and there is not necessarily a clear point at which a question has been answered completely. It may be true that many philosophical questions are complicated and difficult to answer. And because of this difficulty, philosophers may not have given "complete" answers to such questions; but this does not mean they have not made contributions to an answer or progressed toward an answer.

In addition, part of answering a question is discovering which potential answers are wrong. For example, part of determining who committed a certain crime is eliminating potential suspects, showing that likely perpetrators did not in fact commit the crime. While eliminating suspects would not be considered an answer to who committed the crime, it is certainly progress toward an answer. As you learn more about the history of philosophy and philosophical issues in general, you will see that much of the progress toward answering philosophical questions occurs in this manner.

Even if there is some sense in which philosophical questions may be unanswerable or unprovable, this is true of many disciplines. For example, astrophysicists seek to know how old the universe is, how it started, how it became what it is. Given that none of us were present to observe this event (as if one could simply *observe* such a profound event), it may be impossible to know for certain the answer. But astrophysicists will try; they accumulate evidence and put forth answers with evidence to support the answers. As they obtain more evidence, these answers may change or become more precise. Historians may never know for certain who was behind the killing of President John F. Kennedy, who was involved in the planning and execution of his assassination. Is the question unanswerable? To an extent it may be; perhaps most historical questions are, depending on what kind of evidence one requires. But we can certainly narrow the question to certain potential answers and attempt to put forth evidence for one of them. Examples like these abound throughout disciplines that seek answer to questions; thus, it turns out that all disciplines are likely to have questions that are difficult or impossible, *in some sense*, to answer completely.

In general, it is a mistake to characterize philosophy as the study of the unanswerable or unprovable, especially since this is often said in a pejorative sense. Philosophers are trying to give answers to questions; they believe answers can be given. They recognize that the questions they entertain are very difficult to answer, or at least that it is difficult to form a consensus on what the correct answer is. But this does not imply that answers cannot be and have not been given. It merely implies that knowledge in some areas may be more difficult to obtain.

(5) Secularized Religion

I have heard some people characterize philosophy as something like "religion minus God," or secularized religion. The meaning of such a claim is not entirely clear since religion tends to be understood as a deity-based institution with secularism as its opposite. To the extent that we can make sense of this characterization, it conceives of philosophy as an attempt to explain how the world works without any appeals to God, including things such as the origins of the universe and of humans, moral right and wrong, the purpose of life, and so forth.

This understanding of philosophy is simply wrong for a number of reasons. First, as we look through this history of philosophy, we see that a good number of philosophers, if not the majority, not only believed in God and understood such belief to be compatible with their theories, but also developed theories that depended on the existence of God. Readers who are familiar with Rene Descartes' (1596–1650) theory of knowledge in the *Meditations* will recognize this to be a classic example of such dependence.[2] We may certainly debate the quality of philosophy that results from such efforts; however, the point is that philosophy is not necessarily devoid of discussion of God as this characterization would imply. Nor should you think that the only discussion of God by philosophers comes in the form

---

2   Descartes attempts to lay a foundation to our knowledge, a foundation that will justify our claims to know. While he acknowledges that the senses play an important role in what we know, he also recognizes that the senses are fallible. Because they are fallible, we cannot completely trust them and so they are an inadequate foundation. On the basis of principles of reason, he argues for the existence of God, from which he concludes that God would not have created us to be deceived by the senses. Thus we are, in general, justified in our claims to knowledge based on the senses.

of attempts to disprove the existence of God. On the contrary, there is a long history of attempts by philosophers to prove the existence of God.[3]

Second, and more important, it simply is not the case that all the topics and concerns of religion are the topics and concerns of philosophy, or vice versa. In some cases they may overlap, but otherwise the two remain relatively distinct. To put the matter succinctly, if you examine the questions of philosophy (as we will do in Chapter 2), very few of them would be thought of as religious questions. So while it may be true that many philosophers do not believe in God, it does not follow that they take as their purpose to explain the world without God in it, to do what religion attempts to do but without appeal to God.

Finally, one area in which philosophy seems most vulnerable to the claim that it is "secularized religion" is in ethics, the study of moral right and moral wrong. But this supposed tension typically stems from a problematic view of the relationship between God and morality. The view, called "divine command ethics," maintains that what *makes* an action right or wrong is that God commands us to do or not to do it. This view has major problems; primarily that it leaves open the question: why does God command the way he does, for example, why does he command not to kill? The most natural answer is that he commands as he does on the basis of what is independently morally right and morally wrong. It is because killing is morally wrong that God commands not to kill. But if this is the case, then what makes killing morally wrong cannot be that God commands not to kill, for such a claim would be blatantly circular. To avoid the circularity, and maintain the more plausible view, we must conclude that moral right and moral wrong are independent of God's commandments, though some of his commandments (not necessarily all) may be given in virtue of what is morally right and morally wrong.

From this very brief analysis of a complicated subject, it follows that the investigation into moral right and moral wrong—something philosophers indeed do—is not competing with the authority of God's commandments. Rather, it is complementing it. While there is much more to be said about this topic, the important point is that one need not see the philosophers'

---

3 Three of the classical proofs for the existence of God are the ontological proof, the argument from design, and the cosmological proof. One of the classical proofs against the existence of God is the problem of evil.

inquiry into morality as competing with or supplanting religious belief.[4] Thus, the latter should not be taken as support for the view of philosophy as secularized religion.

The Love of Wisdom

We've considered some incorrect characterizations of philosophy, each of which has a kernel of truth and may describe some part of philosophy or some characteristic of philosophical inquiry. None approaches the essence of philosophy or gives an answer to what philosophy is as a whole. Now we will consider an attempt to answer the question in a somewhat straightforward and rhetorically compelling manner. This answer is one of the most common—and I believe worst—answers to the question *what is philosophy*. This common answer is that philosophy is *the love of wisdom*. The reason for giving this answer lies in the etymology of the word "philosophy." The word "philosophy" comes from Greek for "love of wisdom." Specifically, "Philo" comes from Greek for *love* (also found in words like "Philadelphia" and "philanthropy"), and "sophy" comes from Greek for *wisdom* (also found in words like "sophomoric" and "sophistry"). Therefore, one can conclude, philosophy is the love of wisdom. I'll spend the rest of this chapter detailing, and hoping to convince you, why this is such a poor answer.[5]

Problem 1: The answer is descriptively flawed

There is a certain rhetorical appeal to describing oneself as studying the "love of wisdom"; it sounds appropriate because it expresses the etymology of the word. But from the start, the answer seems to be what I call "descriptively" flawed; that is, it only sort of describes philosophy, and even then not accurately. One expects, if anything, that philosophy would be

---

4   One of the earliest challenges to divine command ethics is found in Plato's *Euthyphro*. This dialogue, representing the views of Socrates, entertains the question *what is piety?*

5   The view of philosophy as the love of wisdom does not come merely from the etymology of "philosophy." Among early philosophers such as Socrates and even Plato, there was an especially strong focus on ethics, on how to live one's life well. If wisdom is knowledge of how to live well, philosophy would be the love or pursuit of such wisdom. However, the contemporary teaching of philosophy as *the love of wisdom* is typically justified on the basis of mere etymology.

the *search* for something. Philosophers are seekers, just like physicists, psychologists, and linguists. Philosophers seek answers to questions. To call philosophers "lovers" or philosophy the "love of ..." seems misleading and odd. In particular, we expect not a state-of-being verb, but an active verb; a verb that denotes *doing something*.

It might be objected: but if you love something, like wisdom, then you will seek after it. Two problems arise here. One, this simply doesn't seem to be the case. Humans are not perfectly rational creatures: we can love something and still not pursue it just as we can believe in an ideal and fall short of it. But more to the point, why couch an explanation of what philosophy is in terms of a possible motive for it, in terms of metaphorical language? If anything, all such language accomplishes is to distort and obfuscate what philosophers actually do.

In addition to the oddity of the word "love," the word "wisdom" seems descriptively out of place. In English, "wisdom" denotes practical knowledge for the successful guidance of one's life. While some of philosophy may involve advice for life—and some philosophers certainly exemplified and promoted thoughtful, wise living—it is hardly focused on this advice exclusively or even to a significant degree (as we will see in Chapter Two).[6] Perhaps we could instead understand, in place of "wisdom," something more general like "knowledge." Philosophy would then be understood as something like the *search for knowledge*. This revised answer certainly seems better than *love of wisdom*, but it also is problematic, which we will see as we continue.

Problem 2: The answer is minimally informative

The answer the *love of wisdom*, or its improved form the *search for knowledge*, is hardly informative. Imagine that you have asked someone what philosophy is and they give you this answer. Have you been given a meaningful and informative answer? Do you understand any better what philosophers do as opposed to persons in other disciplines? I suspect not. Part of the problem stems from a general unfamiliarity with philosophy that most people have. For example, most people study mathematics throughout their educations. If someone said that mathematics is the *study of numbers*,

---

6   This aspect of philosophy is certainly emphasized throughout Plato's Republic in which the philosopher is one with a commitment to knowledge and a life guided by such knowledge.

those few words alone will likely appear meaningful and informative given that most people have significantly studied numbers and their properties. But in the case of philosophy—where those who ask "what is philosophy" are probably doing so from near total lack of familiarity—we don't have that sort of advantage.

Worse, the *love of wisdom* or *search for knowledge* describes all sorts of intellectual disciplines. Physicists search for knowledge, sociologists search for knowledge, chemists search for knowledge, historians search for knowledge, and so forth. Any of these people can be described as "searchers of knowledge" and to a lesser degree "lovers of wisdom." But physicists, sociologists, chemists, and historians are not philosophers: when a chemist is mixing chemicals, he or she is not doing philosophy. And when a philosopher talks about moral right and wrong, he or she is not doing physics. While there are respects in which all these disciplines are related (we will discuss this in Chapter Three)—and all involve the search for knowledge—the fact is they are significantly different and that difference needs to be reflected in a correct characterization of philosophy. Just like the characterization of philosophy as deep thinking, philosophy as the love of wisdom or the search for knowledge is too broad to be meaningful.

Problem 3: It answers the wrong question

The third problem is the reasoning for the answer. Frankly, *love of wisdom* seems to be answering the wrong question. The question is "what is philosophy?" The question is not "what does the word 'philosophy' mean?" Suppose you asked me "What is Nevada?" and I answered "it comes from Spanish for 'covered in snow.'" You would likely find this answer very odd. Surely you would expect me to say: it is a state in the United States, located next to California, Utah, and Arizona, it has legalized gambling, and so forth. To tell someone that it is named after a Spanish word is to say something about the name "Nevada"; it is not to say what Nevada, the state, is. The answer *love of wisdom* seems however to do just this, to answer a question about the word "philosophy" rather than tell us something about philosophy itself.

Problem 4: It is the wrong answer to the wrong question

Even if the question we were asking was "what does the word 'philosophy' mean," the answer *love of wisdom* is a mistaken answer. A word's etymology is not synonymous with its meaning. Though the etymology of a word (an account of the words from other languages that it is derived from) may give some clue as to the meaning of the word, it need not. Consider the word "pedophile." This comes from Greek for "children" (pedo) and "love" (philo). So, would you call yourself, if you love children, a pedophile? Surely not. The word "pedophile" refers to someone who has, and indulges, a perverse sexual attraction toward children. Sometimes the etymology of a word will correspond closely to the meaning of the word, and at other times not. A hemophiliac, for example, refers to a person with a serious blood disorder in which the blood does not clot. It does not mean, as the etymology indicates, someone who loves blood. Anyone who has seen a hippopotamus would not describe it as a water horse, despite its etymology.

It is true that etymologies sometimes correspond to or suggest meaning. When new words are introduced into a language, they frequently have some etymological grounding. But for those who insist on appealing to etymology, then "love of wisdom" surely begs for more. The word "love" is after all full of ambiguity: there is brotherly love, romantic love, erotic love, and so forth. So which is correct? Should we now turn to the etymology of the word "love" to answer this question? In general, the etymological approach is a non-starter to answering a "what is" question. It may be helpful at times, but not necessarily so.

It turns out that if we want to know what philosophy is, we will have to look at philosophy itself. We cannot look at the meaning of the word "philosophy" or its etymology. These might give us some direction in understanding what philosophy is, but they hardly give us an adequate answer. As with the other answers we considered, however, this mistaken characterization is not totally unreasonable. As we discuss the history of philosophy in Chapter Three, and again in Chapter Four, we'll discuss briefly how this answer has some, albeit inadequate, justification.

Conclusions

Characterizing philosophy is a difficult thing to do. It is probably difficult to characterize any discipline in a succinct and meaningful way, but with philosophy the problem is especially acute. Most students have exposure, through their secondary education, to a variety of disciplines such as math, science of various types, history, literature, government, and so forth.

Because of this exposure, they can characterize these disciplines with some degree of accuracy or at least have some idea of what they are about. But students typically have little or no experience with philosophy until college. Further, it turns out that philosophy is a very diverse discipline (as we will see in Chapter Two) and has a dramatically evolving character that continues to relate back to its history (as we will see in Chapter Three). Thus, it is difficult to give a two-minute answer to what philosophy is that would be meaningful to one who is not already significantly familiar with it. Many people who ask the question seem to expect quick answer, and I don't believe it's possible to give one in a way that would be informative. With this in mind, we'll turn to the next chapter and make some positive progress toward answering the question of what philosophy is.

Chapter Two

The Parts of Philosophy

What Is Questions

We discussed in the preceding chapter some things that philosophy is not. How shall we go about answering the question in a positive manner? Let's start by considering how we should answer a "what is" question. Here we can find direction from one of the early and great philosophers, Aristotle (384–322 BC). Consider the following example: Mercury is the planet in our solar system that is closest to the Sun. This statement places *Mercury* in the category of *planet in our solar system*, and distinguishes it from other things in the category (other planets) by its being *closest to the Sun*. Aristotle termed these three aspects of classification the "species," "genus," and "differentia," respectively. Many are familiar with the terms "genus" and "species" from the classification schemes used by biologists, though fewer may realize that they originated with Aristotle. For our purposes we can understand these terms as follows:

> *species*: a member or subcategory of the genus (example: *Mercury*)
>
> *genus*: a category (example: *planet in our solar system*)
>
> *differentia*: the characteristics that distinguish one species from another (example: *closest to the Sun*)

Consider *British Columbia*. This belongs to the category *provinces of Canada*. That is to say, *British Columbia* is a member of the category *provinces of Canada*. There are other members of the category *provinces of Canada*: *Ontario, Manitoba, Alberta*, and so forth. The differentia is that which distinguishes British Columbia from Ontario, Manitoba, Alberta and other Canadian provinces. Perhaps the differentia of British Columbia is something like *the southwestern-most province bordering on the Pacific Ocean, the United States, Alberta, and the Yukon and Northwest territories.*

This method of categorization gives us a very effective method for understanding and answering a "what is" question. If one asks "what is a dog," a typical answer will be "an animal." This answer has specified the category to which dogs, the subcategory, belong; they belong to the category of *animal*. Is this a good answer to the question "what is a dog"? In some respects it is. Think of all the things in the universe. If we know that dogs are animals, then we know that dogs are not planets, stars, plants, buildings, cities, and so forth. In many cases, responding with the category to a "what is" question is an adequate answer. If asked "what is the Andromeda?", the answer "a galaxy" might be an adequate answer depending on the purpose in asking the question or depending on how much the inquirer wants to know. On the other hand, sometimes identifying the category is not by itself adequate. Returning to our example of the dog, we know that a cat is also an animal, so is a raccoon, and a pig, and yet these things are not dogs. So more is needed for a complete answer to "what is a dog" than merely "an animal." Namely, we need to specify the differentia, the characteristic or characteristics that distinguish dogs from other things in the category of animal. In the case of dogs, this is the job of the zoologist. Crudely, however, we can say that dogs are animals that bark and are "man's best friend."

Probably the most famous instantiation of this method is attributed to Aristotle in his characterization of man. His characterization: man (the species/subcategory) is the rational (differentia) animal (the genus/category).

In sum, our method for answering a "what is *x*" question is fairly simple:

1. Think of *x* as either a member or subcategory of some broader category.
2. Determine the category to which *x* belongs.

3. Determine what distinguishes *x* from other members or subcategories of the category.[1]

It is sometimes easier to accomplish (2) by thinking about the many things that are associated with *x*, the things that we think of as being grouped together with *x*. For example, suppose we ask "What is copper?" To answer this, we think of copper as a subcategory of some broader category, and then ask: what is the broader category that it belongs to? We tend to associate copper with things like iron, nickel, aluminum, and these things are *metals*. Now we move to step (3): what distinguishes copper from other metals? Precisely answering this is the job of the chemist, who might point out that it has 29 protons in its nucleus. But we can at least say the following: it is a metal that is especially conductive of electricity, ductile, malleable, and has an orange-like coloring.

Applying the Method to Philosophy

We can now apply this method to our question "what is philosophy" by first identifying the category to which philosophy belongs. What things do we see philosophy associated with? Philosophy is generally conducted at the modern university with things like physics, biology, literature studies, linguistics, psychology, anthropology, and so forth. And what are these things? They are disciplines: well-defined areas of inquiry and study.

This is a good start. Philosophy (the subcategory/species) is a discipline (the category/genus). We can even be a bit more specific and say that philosophy is an *intellectual* discipline. Why do we add this? Disciplines have various outcomes. Some disciplines—engineering, for example—have as their outcome a *physical product*. The engineer produces buildings, roads, machines, and so forth. Engineers may not physically build them, but they contribute in an essential way to their design. Similarly, musicians have,

---

1   As biologists have done with classifications of life, and as Aristotle himself discusses, the genus/species distinction can be multiplied for any purposes. Thus, in asking what Denver is, we can say it belongs to the category cities in Colorado, which itself belongs to the category cities in America, which belongs to the category cities. Within the category cities in Colorado, we distinguish it from other cities in Colorado by its being the capital. Depending on how finely one wishes to categorize something—and so characterize it in greater detail—one will make use of additional categories and subcategories.

as the outcome of their discipline, a product (a musical work, a musical composition) or a performance. The outcome of philosophy, on the other hand, is knowledge. In this respect philosophers are similar to physicists, astronomers, political scientists, mathematicians, economists: the outcome of these disciplines is knowledge. The knowledge may be used by others for various purposes—the knowledge can be applied—but the disciplines themselves aim at knowledge. Hence philosophy is not just a *discipline*, but an *intellectual discipline*.[2]

In claiming that philosophy is an intellectual discipline we should not understand this as meaning that philosophers are particularly smart, that the discipline is especially difficult, or that the conclusions are pointless or "merely academic." The term "intellectual" is not being used in any pejorative or specialized sense (i.e., it is not being used in the sense that we speak of someone as an "intellectual"). It merely means "aimed at knowledge." Further, you might ask "don't engineers aim at better understanding or knowledge of materials so that they can produce better products? So aren't they intellectual disciplines in that sense?" It is certainly true that engineers, and researchers in engineering, aim to produce knowledge. But it is done with the aim of producing products. The aim of producing products is not evident in intellectual disciplines. Furthermore, although a biochemist may hope that her research leads to the development of new drugs, for example, the role of such development belongs to the engineer, not the biochemist. The biochemist produces the knowledge that others can use. Finally, note that individual practitioners of a discipline may be involved in many undertakings. Though philosophy aims at producing knowledge, most philosophers are academics who teach philosophy to students in addition to doing philosophy. Likewise, there may be chemists who, in addition to discovering knowledge about molecules, actively work to bring about products based on their research. In that sense they are acting both as chemists and engineers.

We now have the first part of our answer, the category or genus to which philosophy belongs: philosophy is an intellectual discipline. But there are many other intellectual disciplines: geology, biology, linguistics, chemistry, psychology, and so forth. What distinguishes philosophy from them? To

---

2   To be sure, many disciplines, or practitioners of disciplines, may have mixed outcomes. Certain engineers may have as their aim not merely products but also knowledge about how to produce better products.

answer this question, let's start with a more general question: what distinguishes any intellectual discipline from another? There seems to be two good answers to this question: an intellectual discipline is distinguished by (1) its subject matter, and (2) the questions it asks.

First, we might think that one intellectual discipline differs from another by its subject matter. At risk of oversimplifying, let's consider a few examples. The subject matter of mathematics is numbers, the subject matter of psychology is the mind and behavior, the subject matter of chemistry is substances and their properties. This is a good answer to what distinguishes disciplines, but sometimes two disciplines appear to have the same subject matter but ask different questions about the subject matter. For example, both human physiology and kinesiology study the human body, but they ask different questions about it. Kinesiology considers how the human body moves. Human physiology considers how the human body as a whole functions, in particular by looking at the various systems of the human body.

It might be objected that kinesiology and human physiology do have different subject matters; the answer "the human body" merely underspecifies the subject matter. Indeed, this may be a valid point. Either way, the risk of underspecification is more easily avoided with the second answer: disciplines differ in virtue of the questions they ask. Questions like "how does the human body move" and "how does the human body function" are distinct while at the same time revealing a similar object of study. In the end, both of these answers have advantages, though the second gives us a method for more precisely determining the first: by considering the questions that the practitioners of an intellectual discipline ask, we can effectively distinguish its subject matter from that of others.

The Questions of Philosophy

To distinguish philosophy from other intellectual disciplines we need to consider the questions it asks. As it turns out, philosophy encompasses an extremely diverse set of questions. This point cannot be emphasized enough: the questions of philosophy are so diverse that the discipline nearly appears to lack coherency. Furthermore, philosophers tend to group these questions according to certain classifications that are, in effect, *subdisciplines* of philosophy. Let's consider several major subdisciplines and the questions they ask, namely: metaphysics, epistemology, logic, ethics, philosophy of language, and philosophy of mind. I note that our brief consideration of these subdisciplines is intended to be complete or detailed. We are considering these only with the aim of understanding philosophy as a whole.

Epistemology

Epistemology is the study of knowledge. This includes questions such as *what is knowledge, how does knowledge differ from mere opinion, what constitutes adequate justification for a belief to be considered knowledge, is all knowledge based on the senses?* Once again, a contrast with other disciplines is in order. Researchers in many fields seek to gain knowledge. Astrophysicists seek knowledge or understanding of the make-up of the universe. Economists seek to know how changes in the economic policies of nations will affect world markets. Historians want to know how events in the past were brought about, and how they influenced other events including current events. Further, ordinary persons seek knowledge: I wish to know if there is an accident on the freeway before I enter the on-ramp. Philosophers, however, seek to understand knowledge in general: they seek to understand what knowledge itself is.

An example of a classical epistemological debate concerns the justification of knowledge. Empiricists, such as David Hume (1711–1776), believed that all knowledge is based on sensory observation. Rationalists, such as Rene Descartes (1596 –1650), believed that some knowledge is based on something other than sensory observation. The prime candidate for such non-empirical knowledge is reason. That is, our rational, thinking capabilities lay the foundation for some of our knowledge.

Metaphysics

Metaphysics can be characterized as the study of the general nature of reality or existence. Many disciplines entertain existence questions. For example, a marine biologist might ask *what kinds of animals, if any, exist at the deepest parts of the ocean.* An astronomer might ask *do black holes exist,* as predicted by Einstein's theory of general relativity. But philosophers ask far more general questions such as *do properties* (such as the property of being red, or being happy) *exist,* and *what kinds of objects exist besides physical objects* (abstract objects). Further, philosophers inquire into the nature of things that exist, again at a very general level. Consider numbers. We talk about numbers. Just as I may say to you "My brother is my favorite person," I can say to you "The number 8 is my favorite number." My brother is a physical object. I can see him, hear him, and interact with him. What about the number 8? What kind of an object is it? Apparently, it is some sort of an object, perhaps an abstract object. It is surely not something we see. And this leads to the philosophical question: *how do abstract objects differ from physical objects.*

Another question of metaphysics concerns the characteristics of cause and effect (causation); for, we believe that physical objects are interrelated causally. Once again, it is useful to contrast a philosopher's concern with causation from that of other researchers. A climatologist might ask what causes hurricanes, or might debate whether or not CO_2 emissions cause global warming. Medical researchers want to better understand what causes cancer. Philosophers, however, are not concerned with particular cases of causation; they seek to understand causation in general. What does it mean to say that one thing causes another? How are we to characterize and understand causation? Are there general principles of causation that we can formulate?

Logic

Logic is the study of inference, and philosophers usually consider these inferences in the form of arguments. Consider the following argument:

(1) All dogs are mammals.

(2) Some dogs are unfriendly.

Therefore, (3) some unfriendly things are mammals.

This is certainly a good argument. But philosophers are not concerned with particular arguments like this. Rather, they are concerned with arguments in general, with the form of inference that takes place in good arguments as opposed to bad arguments. In the above example, we can exhibit the form of inference as follows:

(1) All A is B

(2) Some A is C

Therefore, (3) Some C is B.

As it turns out, any argument that fits this form will be a good argument; the inference from (1) and (2) to (3) is a valid inference.

Philosophers have progressed in their study of logic well beyond what this simple example shows. Once again, logic bears similarities to some characteristics of metaphysics and epistemology. First, making inferences is something that we do as ordinary persons, not just researchers and academics. We do this on a regular basis. If my stomach hurts and I have not eaten any food, I infer that I'm hungry. If my stomach hurts and I have eaten food and a stomach flu is going around, I may infer that I'm sick. Second, philosophers are not interested in particular arguments, but in argumentation in general. *What in general makes for a good argument (or good inference)? What principles of good arguments can we formulate? When does an argument constitute a proof?*

Ethics

Ethics is the study of how we should live our lives, though most ethical discussion tends to focus on the particular issues of morality: morally right and wrong actions, and morally good and bad things. Philosophers ask a variety of questions with regard to this subject. Some are very general: what does it *mean* to say an action is right or wrong, and what *makes* an action right or wrong? For example, we suppose that certain actions are wrong such as physically harming another person for the fun of it. But what is it about these actions that makes them wrong? What property do they have in common such that we consider them wrong and, therefore, actions we ought not to do?[3] In asking this question, the moral philosopher is not being a skeptic. He or she is not asking in the sense of "prove it to me or I won't believe it." Rather, harming another for the fun of it is taken to be a given for which the philosopher wishes to give an explanation. The moral philosopher is in the same position as the chemist who tries to explain why

---

3   Two of the classical theories of moral right and more wrong are called Utilitarianism and Deontology. The former postulates that an action is morally right or wrong depending on the consequences of the action, in particular, how much happiness it promotes. John Stuart Mill's aptly titled Utilitarianism is a fairly straightforward development of this kind of theory. The latter kind of theory maintains that actions are right or wrong in and of themselves, not necessarily in virtue of their consequences. The Groundwork of the Metaphysics of Morals, by Immanuel Kant, is best representative of this kind of theory.

iron rusts. That iron rusts under certain circumstances is a given; the task of inquiry is to determine why it rusts, not dispute that it rusts.

As part of understanding what makes an action morally wrong, philosophers have also tried to understand the nature of action in general. If we can understand the form that action takes—what distinguishes rational action from mere animal behavior—then perhaps we can better understand moral action. This inquiry into action includes questions of free will: *are we free in our actions? can we demonstrate it? If we are free, how would that fit, if it fits, with the view that the world is determined?* Sometimes this kind of inquiry is referred to as *Philosophy of Action*.

Some questions in ethics are fairly particular. Philosophers, especially recently, have rigorously pursued questions that might be termed "applied ethics." These are still questions related to right and wrong, but of a far more particular nature. For example, philosophers have discussed extensively the morality of abortion, our obligations to the third-world poor, the rights of animals, and so forth. In these cases, philosophers have attempted to arrive at answers about a particular kind of action and its moral standing.

Philosophy of Language

Philosophy of language seeks to understand how language functions at its most fundamental level. Consider the following two groups of symbols: "xb—y!yysy" and "George Washington." The first group of symbols is meaningless whereas the second is meaningful. Given that both of these groups of symbols are, on the surface, merely markings on the book page, there is a genuine question as to how they are so different: how the first group of symbols represents nothing and the second represents George Washington. Philosophers of language are generally not concerned with more empirical matters such as how we acquire language, how language is best taught, or the differences in various languages. These are issues studied by linguists. Philosophers are concerned with how the words a person uses—given that he or she has learned a language, and has the various capacities necessary for language—represent the world and express his or her thoughts. Another question studied by philosophers of language is truth. We think of some sentences as true: "the Earth is round," and others as not true, "2 plus 2 is 7." But what is it to say that a sentence is true or not true? Again, two points are worth emphasis. One, the philosopher is not being a skeptic about truth in asking such a question; he or she wants to know how truth works. Two, the philosopher is not concerned with particular truths. He or she is concerned with what truth is in general.

Understanding language is particularly important for philosophers because an understanding of language is critical for doing philosophy well. How so? If you consider the above set of questions, they are for the most part non-empirical. They are questions that do not require observation, the use of our senses. Philosophers do not work in a laboratory, do surveys, or collect social data for computation and inference. Philosophical inquiry tends to be conceptual. All this is to say that the medium in which much of philosophy is done—in which philosophical experiment and discovery takes place—is language. You might say that language is the laboratory of philosophy. Because of this, a correct understanding of language is especially important to philosophers.[4]

Philosophy of Mind

Philosophy of mind concerns the nature of the mental. Note that the psychologist also studies the mental, but in a different way. A psychologist may study, for example, how a person's self-esteem (belief in one's own worth) affects his or her happiness. But philosophers are concerned to understand what a mere belief is; they are not concerned with any particular beliefs. Furthermore, philosophers are concerned to understand in general the nature of other mental states: desires, perceptions, conceptualizations, and so forth.[5]

Another major concern of the philosophy of mind is the relationship between the mind and the physical world. To the extent that we have minds, we think of them as causing actions (mental causation): my belief that I'm hungry causes me to go to the refrigerator and get some food. But how does the mind interact with the physical world? Is the mind a non-physical sort of substance, as it in some sense appears to be? Is the mind merely the brain? This classical problem of philosophy is called

---

4   An example of a classical problem of philosophy of language is the problem of negative existentials: the problem of denying the existence of something. Suppose I say "round squares do not exist." Everyone agrees that this is true. But the question what are we talking about arises. If the statement is true, then round squares don't exist. But if they don't exist, then how can they be the subject of the sentence?

5   As with many disciplines, there may be significant overlapping. For example, issues in areas of psychology like cognitive psychology and theoretical psychology may overlap with philosophical issues in the philosophy of mind.

the mind–body problem.[6] Philosophers of mind are also concerned to understand nature of conscious, first-person experience (this is sometimes referred to as phenomenology).

Metaphysics, epistemology, logic, ethics, philosophy of language, and philosophy of mind are some, but not all, of the major subdisciplines of philosophy. Our characterization of them has been brief and abridged. Some other subdisciplines of philosophy and their questions include:

Philosophy of Religion: What is the nature of religious belief? What is faith? Can we prove the existence of God, and what particular proofs or arguments for his existence can we give? Is the existence of God compatible with the suffering we observe in the world?

Philosophy of Science: What is the nature of scientific method and progress? How are we to understand and integrate into our worldview the conclusions of science? How are we to understand certain scientific peculiarities such as quantum mechanics and relativity theory? What is the nature of space and time?

Political Philosophy: What justifies societal authority? What kind of government is best? What should the aim of government be? What constitutes societal justice? What distribution of societal goods is fair?

The Problem

Now that we have some exposure to the parts of philosophy, to the questions it asks, we have a new problem. This set of philosophical questions is incredibly diverse; more diverse, I would hazard to say, than any other intellectual discipline (and by a long shot). One subdiscipline of philosophy is concerned with existence, another is concerned with knowledge, yet another is concerned with words and their functioning, still another is concerned with right and wrong behavior, and action in general. Another is concerned with God and religious belief, another with arguments. That these questions may overlap with one another (and with other disciplines)

---

6 Thomas Nagel, for example, argues in "What Is It Like to Be a Bat?" that the nature of conscious mental experience—like the experience of seeing red—cannot be reduced to a physical description; that is, that no physical description could characterize what red is like. Because of this, the mind–body problem cannot presently be solved by attempting to show that all mental phenomena are really just physical phenomena such as brain states.

does not make the problem any easier. For example, one issue about right and wrong is how we know right and wrong, so there are epistemic questions in the area of ethics. But this doesn't serve to unify our understanding of ethics and epistemology; in fact it may further complicate it. So despite the frequent overlap of philosophical questions, these subdisciplines appear to have extremely different subject matters.

One might suggest that we answer our question of what philosophy is as follows: philosophy is an intellectual discipline that asks what kinds of objects exist, what is causation, what is knowledge, what is right and wrong, what is action (and we continue until we have listed all philosophical questions). But this seems like a lame approach. While it includes the many questions that philosophers discuss—and indeed it is essential that we understand and recognize the diversity of questions in philosophy—we also need to understand what unifies these diverse questions of philosophy into one discipline. What is it about all these questions that is so similar that they should be regarded as one discipline? By determining what unifies these philosophical questions, we will be in effect characterizing what philosophy is. To this end we will turn to the next chapter and give a first answer: what unifies the diverse questions of philosophy is its history.

Chapter Three

The History of Philosophy

W e finished the preceding chapter with a basic understanding of some philosophical questions but also with a concern for what unifies these diverse questions. In this chapter we will briefly learn about the history of philosophy for two reasons: one, an understanding of the history of philosophy will serve to unify the diversity we find in the discipline, and so help to answer our question of what philosophy is as a whole. Two, philosophy, unlike many disciplines, continues to be heavily invested in its history. Contemporary philosophers address past philosophers as sources of understanding, as continuing participants in the discussions that continue to this day. So, for example, one question in the area of free will is the following: is free will compatible with a deterministic world? Aptly named "compatibilists" affirm this question: the universe can be determined while at the same time allowing that persons possess free will. "Incompatibilists" deny this. In addressing this philosophical debate, one might very well discuss the writings and arguments of Immanuel Kant (1724–1804), who addresses this very tension, even though his writings are over 200 years old. Therefore, a familiarity with the history of philosophy is essential to a fuller understanding of what philosophy is and how philosophy is conducted.

Before we start, we should make a few qualifications. First, while the history of philosophy is part of what unifies the diverse questions of philosophy, and this aspect is a necessary part of any correct characterization of philosophy; it ultimately, by itself, provides an unsatisfactory answer. We will conclude the chapter by discussing why this answer is unsatisfactory. In the next chapter, we will discuss why this answer is nevertheless an essential component to a correct characterization of philosophy.

Second, the historical themes, figures, and ideas we will consider in this chapter are far from complete. Any attempt to deeply understand the history of philosophy surely must involve reading the actual writings of past philosophers. My aim in this chapter, however, is to present a big-picture view of the history of philosophy that will be adequate for our introductory and holistic purposes. For those who are familiar with philosophy, and for those who are new to it, this will be more than adequate.

Third, the philosophical figures and movements that we will review here are those of Western culture and history; one might say we are considering only "Western Philosophy." There are two reasons for this. First, the discussion of topics that began with the ancient Greeks (as we will see below) have formed the most cohesive, sustained, and prolific discussions in our intellectual history. Because of this, most contemporary philosophical discussion and theorizing draw upon and have grown from this tradition. Second, our purpose is to review the most important and widely recognized figures in philosophy. There are many that are being left out from the Western tradition in addition to other traditions. None of this is to suggest that important philosophical ideas have not been discussed or considered in various cultures and at various times.

Timeline of Philosophy

Philosophy can be roughly grouped into four historical periods: ancient, medieval, modern, and contemporary. For each of these periods, I have listed several major philosophers, the dates of their lives, and some major views or works of theirs. These lists are important primarily for the sake of familiarity: you may recognize a few (depending on how much philosophy you have studied). If you are new to philosophy, you may recognize none at all. They are provided to promote familiarity with the major philosophical figures and periods.

Ancient Philosophy

The Pre-Socratics

> *Thales:* (c. 625–c. 545 BC) water is the basic element of the universe, reputed to have predicted solar eclipse
>
> *Pythagoras:* (c. 570–c. 490 BC) theories of mathematics, Pythagorean theorem
>
> *Parmenides:* (c. 515–c. 445 BC) skepticism about change/motion
>
> *Anaxagoras:* (c. 500–c. 428 BC) "Mind" as the moving force of the physical world
>
> *Heraclitus:* (c. 540–c. 480 BC) physical world is constantly changing, fire is the basic element
>
> *Empedocles:* (c. 484–c. 430 BC) reality as four elements: water, air, fire, earth
>
> *Democritus:* (c. 470–c. 360 BC) atomist, ethicist
>
> *Zeno of Elea:* (c. 490–c. 430 BC) arguments against Pythagorean beliefs in plurality, motion (Zeno's paradoxes)

Despite the name "*pre*-Socratics," most of these early philosophers were contemporaries of Socrates. They are typically recognized as the earliest group of philosophers, and they lived in the area of ancient Greece. Surely others, in Greece and elsewhere, asked philosophical questions before or at the same time as the pre-Socratics. However, our earliest records of philosophical thought are from the pre-Socratics. In addition, their theorizing captured the attention of others who responded to, challenged, and developed their ideas in a tradition that has continued to this day. Presently, we have very little of the writings of the pre-Socratics: what we have is preserved only in fragmented form, as quoted or reproduced by other authors from antiquity.

Much of what the pre-Socratics were concerned with were questions that today we would call "scientific." Consider, for example, Thales. He postulated that the basic element of the universe was water. This may seem quaint by today's standards where we recognize over 100 elements—you might think "how could someone come up with a theory that is so obviously false?" But if we put ourselves in Thales' perspective, we can see some logic to his view. How so? One reason for theorizing about what things are made up of is to explain change: how one thing changes into another. Further, one way to explain how things change from one thing to another is to postulate that all things are made up of the same thing, just arranged in different forms. Given the fact that water is an essential, abundant, and obvious component of most life forms, it is not so unreasonable—especially for one who does not have the benefit of our contemporary understanding of the world—to think that water might be the basic element that everything is made up of.

> *Socrates*: (470–399 BC) "father" of philosophy, mentor of Plato, left no writings of his own though his views are represented in the early writings of Plato
>
> *Plato*: (c. 428–347 BC) teacher of Aristotle, founder of the Academy, wrote the Socratic dialogues (representing the views of Socrates), as well as his own; wrote on a wide range of philosophical topics including epistemology, metaphysics, ethics, and political philosophy
> * *Republic, The Laws, Timaeus, Euthyphro, Apology, Crito, Phaedo*
>
> *Aristotle*: (384–322 BC) influential theories on logic, metaphysics, epistemology, ethics, politics, rhetoric, biology, anatomy, meteorology, physics, literature, poetry
> * *Nicomachean Ethics, Metaphysics, De Anima, Physics, Posterior Analytics*
>
> *Epicurus*: (341–270 BC) ethicist, pleasure is the highest good
>
> *Plotinus*: (c. 204–270 AD) neoplatonist, reality is beyond the physical world, philosophy helps one to reach this reality
> * *Enneads*

Socrates is typically thought of as the father of philosophy. This is partly because of his influence and partly because he has left, through the writings of his student Plato, many complete discussions of philosophical topics. Much of Socrates' philosophy focuses on what we would term *ethics*. For example, in the *Euthyphro*, Socrates discusses the nature of piety. In the *Crito*, he discusses justice. Socrates' famous student, Plato, continued the tradition of Socrates but expanded his range of topics and the depth of discussion. Plato discoursed on subjects such as love, knowledge, politics, morality, education, and metaphysics. Plato's most famous student, Aristotle, continued to further expand the range of topics to logic, the mind, the motion of the planets (astronomy), literary theory, anatomy, biology, and the weather. Together, Plato and Aristotle were by far the most influential ancient philosophers and many would argue the most influential philosophers ever.

There are three essential points to be aware of with regard to the inception of philosophy among the ancient Greeks. Their importance to properly understanding what philosophy is and its place in our western intellectual tradition cannot be underestimated. First, philosophy arose in opposition to the practice of supernatural explanation. Prior to philosophy, there was a tradition among the Greeks (and elsewhere) of giving explanations for various phenomena in terms of supernatural forces such as, for the Greeks, the Olympian gods. The gods were appealed to not only to explain physical phenomena (such as natural disasters), but also to explain social phenomena (such as war). The works of Homer (*The Iliad, The Odyssey*) and Hesiod (*The Theogony*) exemplify this sort of explanation.

Consider, for example, the supernatural explanation for why we have the seasons. According to the Greek mythology, Persephone was kidnapped by Hades, the god of the underworld. While there, she violated one of the rules of the underworld by eating several pomegranate seeds. As punishment for the prohibition against eating in the underworld, she was committed to remain in the underworld. Her distraught mother, Demeter, the goddess of the harvest, was so sorrowful that she no longer caused the vegetation of the earth to grow. Without food, mankind was on the verge of starvation until Zeus intervened, and she was condemned to spend several months each year in the underworld while being free for the other months. While in the underworld, Demeter, in her sorrow, does not cause the vegetation to grow, corresponding to the fall and winter months. When Persephone is free of the underworld, Demeter then causes the vegetation to grow, corresponding to the spring and summer months.

The early philosophers, however, were cautious with regard to this kind of approach to explanation. The difference is not that they never included the supernatural in their explanations; rather, the supernatural no longer was the *default mode of explanation*. Appeals to supernatural forces became one option among others. So while one might still explain a natural disaster by appealing to the anger of the gods, for example, one might also explain it (and even show it to be a better explanation) by appeal to natural forces. Further, where explanations were given in terms of the supernatural, it was not necessarily according to the traditional understanding of the supernatural. A succinct way to characterize this point is that philosophy (and philosophers) distinguished itself by its attempt to give *rational explanations*. To emphasize, by *rational* we do not mean that these explanations did not include or involve the supernatural—the history of philosophy, including Greek philosophy, has numerous appeals to deity. Rather, the supernatural is merely one option among many in the attempt to give the best explanations and theories of phenomena.

Second, philosophy arose in opposition to sophistry. During the time of Socrates and the pre-Socratics there were in ancient Greece a group of people known as "sophists." The sophists were professional orators who would teach students the art of speaking well. In many cases, they were hired by wealthy Greeks to teach their children. Many of the writings of Plato represent Socrates in dialogue (usually conflict) with the sophists, and the contrast between philosophers and sophists is severe. The sophists were concerned with mere persuasion; they were concerned with getting others to do or believe what they wanted. They were not, as with philosophers, concerned with the truth. This is not to say that a sophist was necessarily attempting to deceive. But his motivating concern was only to *convince* others to adopt his position; his concern was not with its actual correctness. To this day, those who are unfamiliar with philosophy will at times accuse it of being sophistry. I have heard some say, essentially, that philosophy is the art of *verbal trickery*, or, philosophy is all *smoke and mirrors*. Nothing could be farther from the truth; philosophy gets started in distinction from sophistry.[1]

Third, at its inception, philosophy included roughly all areas of intellectual inquiry. Not only did philosophy involve the topics that we covered in the previous chapter, but it also included topics that we would today call "scientific." The best example of this is found in the writings of Aristotle. For example, one of the books that Aristotle wrote is titled *Parts of Animals*. It is a book on anatomy. Another is called *On the Heavens*. It is a book on astronomy. We don't normally think of scientific questions as philosophical questions—certainly not anatomy and astronomy—but at this point

---

1 A classical work showing Socrates in conflict with the Sophists is the Gorgias, named after a famous Greek sophist.

in our Western intellectual tradition they were not distinguished. In this sense the understanding of philosophy as "the love of wisdom," or better "the search for knowledge," has some plausibility. This understanding of philosophy is augmented by the fact that Socrates, at least, was primarily concerned with ethical questions, and many other questions may have been motivated by ethical questions: thus, epistemological questions were motivated by a desire to *know* how to live life.

Medieval Philosophy

> *St. Augustine*: (354–430 AD) philosophy serves to help interpret and understand Christianity, incorporates Platonic, Neoplatonic themes in his philosophy
> ▪ *Confessions, City of God*
>
> *St. Anselm*: (1033–1109) ontological argument for the existence of God; rational analysis of Christianity did not necessarily lead to doubt and loss of faith
> ▪ *Proslogion*
>
> *St. Thomas Aquinas*: (1225–1274) Aristotelianism adapted to Christianity
> ▪ *Summa Theologiae*
>
> *William of Ockham*: (c. 1285–1349) theological approach to epistemology, logic, metaphysics; Ockham's razor

Medieval philosophy is dominated by an interest in Christianity, the Christian church, and its doctrines. Further, the views of ancient philosophers tend to influence medieval philosophers strongly not only in the questions they ask, but also in the answers they give. While the discussions of Medieval philosophy may have started primarily from the desire to understand or explain the principles of the Christian church, the results of such inquiry were often more general and therefore not limited in their relevance merely to the understanding of Christian doctrine.

Modern Philosophy

Francis Bacon: (1561–1626) promoted the advancement of scientific knowledge/natural philosophy
- *The Advancement of Learning, Novum Organum*

Thomas Hobbes: (1588–1679) political philosophy, ethics
- *Leviathan*

Rene Descartes: (1596–1650) beginning of modern philosophical thought; rational method of doubting to discover what cannot be doubted; "Cogito Ergo Sum"
- *Discourse on Method, Meditations on First Philosophy*

Benedictus Spinoza: (1632–1677) universe identical with God who is the uncaused substance; substance is a metaphysical entity, the basis of all reality
- *Ethics*

Gottfried Leibniz: (1646–1716) work in mathematics (infinitesimal calculus), physics (monadic universe), theology, law, politics, history
- *Monadology, New Essays Concerning Human Understanding*

John Locke: (1632–1704) no innate ideas, ideas arise through experience (through the senses), interest in political philosophy, legitimacy of revolution
- *Essay Concerning Human Understanding, Two Treatises of Government*

George Berkeley: (1685–1753) idealist, objects do not exist if they are not perceived
- *A Treatise Concerning the Principles of Human Knowledge*

David Hume: (1711–1776) empiricist, no *a priori* knowledge, morality is not an outgrowth of reason
- *Treatise of Human Nature, An Enquiry Concerning the Human Understanding*

Modern philosophy is typically thought to start with the great French philosopher Rene Descartes. Modern philosophy distinguishes itself from medieval philosophy in a number of ways. First, it is not so exclusively concerned with using philosophy to understand and develop the doctrines of the Christian church (and vice versa). Second, modern philosophy seems very interested in the emerging progress of our understanding of the physical world. These are both very evident in the great work of Descartes, the *Meditations*. Descartes wants to develop a secure foundation for our understanding of the natural world. Note that the great scientist Galileo Galilei lived from 1564–1642, during the time of Descartes. Nicolaus Copernicus lived just before the time of Descartes, from 1473–1543. Thus, modern philosophy came forth during the time of great "scientific" progress. Third, modern philosophy takes a special interest in epistemology, the study of how we know (see Chapter Two). Again, this is related in part to its interest in the emerging understanding the natural, physical world. Their thinking was as follows: in order to avoid the errors of past theorizing, philosophers should first understand how we have knowledge, and in particular how we can know things with certainty. Once that matter is settled, we can further our understanding of the natural world without the worry that our knowledge will, in the future, be shown to be false.

> *Isaac Newton*: (1642–1727) natural philosophy (science, physics); mathematically explained physical phenomena
> • *Mathematical Principles of Natural Philosophy*
>
> *Jean-Jacques Rousseau*: (1712–1778) ethics, social and political philosophy
> • *Emile, Social Contract*
>
> *Immanuel Kant*: (1724–1804) groundbreaking work in metaphysics, epistemology, and ethics
> • *Critique of Pure Reason, Groundwork of the Metaphysics of Morals*

The inclusion of Isaac Newton on this list should come as a surprise because we think of him as a physicist and a scientist, not a philosopher. Although this is correct, it is somewhat misleading because it is during the period of modern philosophy that the sciences begin to break off and distinguish themselves from philosophy. Consider the title of Newton's famous work: *Mathematical Principles of Natural Philosophy*. It is not, as we might expect, "Mathematical Principles of Physics." At this time, as before, questions that we term "scientific" are still considered part of philosophy ("natural philosophy") though they are in the process of emerging into their own disciplines. This trend continues until there become distinct sciences (and social sciences): physics, chemistry, biology, psychology, sociology, economics, anthropology, and so forth. If one wishes to read one of the first psychology books in our Western tradition, then one should look to Aristotle's *De Anima* (meaning "on the soul"), psychology is still a part of philosophy. But by the time of Sigmund Freud, for example, psychology has become its own discipline.

At least two things characterize these emerging disciplines. One, they tend to be empirical—they depend significantly on observation for the greater part of their explanations. Empirical methods may work better with some sciences (the physical or hard sciences) than with others (the social sciences), but these disciplines at least aspire to be empirical. Two, and perhaps because of these empirical methods, the fields of inquiry are very successful at systematically answering the questions they pose. Newton's theory, for example, was extremely successful at answering a wide range of questions and explaining a wide range of phenomena about the motion of objects. This second feature should be qualified (since, as it turns out, for example, Newton's system was wrong). These emerging disciplines were able to garner a wide range of consensus among inquirers: agreement among those in the discipline. In some cases this consensus may be due to the fact that the answers are, to some degree, correct. Nevertheless, the mere ability to reach meaningful consensus in a discipline about certain answers allows the discipline to continue in its development and to entertain and answer further questions.

Contemporary Philosophy

G.W.F. Hegel: (1770–1831) attempted to construct a comprehensive philosophical system encompassing all ideas, past and future; "Absolute Spirit" in process of dialectic self-development
- *Phenomenology of Spirit, Philosophy of Right*

John Stuart Mill: (1806–1873) utilitarian ethics, classical liberal political philosophy
- *On Liberty, Utilitarianism*

Friedrich Nietzsche: (1844–1900) morality based on "will to power" instead of reason
- *Beyond Good and Evil, The Will to Power, Thus Spoke Zarathustra*

Gottlob Frege: (1848–1925) logic, philosophy of mathematics; father of modern logic, modern mathematical logic and philosophical logic, philosophy of language
- *Concept Notation, "On Sense and Nominatum"*

Bertrand Russell: (1872–1970) mathematics can be stated in terms of the concepts of general logic
- *Principia Mathematica (with Alfred North Whitehead), "On Denoting"*

G.E. Moore: (1873–1958) pioneer in linguistic conceptual analysis; "good" is unanalyzable nonnatural concept upon which morality and ethics is built
- *Principia Ethica, "The Refutation of Idealism"*

Martin Heidegger: (1889–1976) developed existential phenomenology
- *Being and Time, Introduction to Metaphysics*

Ludwig Wittgenstein: (1889–1951) philosopher of language
- *Tractatus Logico-Philosophicus, Philosophical Investigations*

W.V.O. Quine: (1908–2000) logician, philosopher of language, criticized distinction of analytic and synthetic statements
- *"Two Dogmas of Empiricism," Word and Object*

Modern philosophy can be thought of as ending around the time of Kant, thus ushering in the period of contemporary philosophy. We will not discuss much historically about contemporary philosophy other than that the breaking away of the sciences that started in the modern period has continued. There are certainly important movements, divisions, and doctrines in contemporary philosophy that are of important interest to philosophers.

The Historical Answer and Its Problems

Now that we have a brief understanding of the history of philosophy, how does this help us to answer the question of what unifies the diverse questions of philosophy? It helps by giving us the following answer: philosophy is an intellectual discipline that initially aimed at knowledge in all areas of inquiry but now is concerned with those areas that are "left over," areas that have not successfully separated into their own disciplines.

This characterization certainly expresses a truth about philosophy and its history. To some degree it solves the unification problem: the reason these diverse questions are in one discipline is that this discipline histori- cally incorporated most intellectual areas of inquiry. But this answer has serious shortcomings. It tells us little about what unifies the remaining ar- eas of philosophy other than we have not been successful in systematically answering their questions or in coming to a consensus on putative answers. This seems to be a disappointingly less-than-informative answer to our inquiry. We think, or at least hope, that there is something intrinsic to the questions and inquiries themselves that unifies them. We seek an answer that will in part explain why the various questions of philosophy, and its diverse subdisciplines, *should* remain together in one coherent discipline. History explains why some parts of philosophy have departed, but not why the remaining parts have stayed together.

As a side note, the historical answer lends some plausibility to the view that philosophy is the study of the unanswerable or unprovable. While this answer is ultimately incorrect (as explained in Chapter One), we can see how someone might think that it correctly characterizes philosophy. Given the enormous success at answering questions, or at least in creating consensus, that we see in some of the sciences—in apparent contrast to philosophy—it is tempting to think of philosophy as the study of unan- swerable or unprovable questions. At the same time, the departure of these disciplines from philosophy undermines the view of philosophy as the unprovable. For, as aspects of philosophy have developed and succeeded in answering questions, they then broke off, thus making the impression that philosophical problems cannot be answered suspect at best.

In sum, the problem with the historical account is that it fails to char- acterize the diverse subdisciplines of philosophy in a positive, informative way. Although we can do better than this in giving an answer to what philosophy is, our time has not been wasted. For this historical aspect of the discipline does play an important role in understanding any character- ization of philosophy. We'll return to it in the next chapter after we have considered a more fruitful understanding of what philosophy is as a whole.

Chapter Four

What Is Philosophy?

Wₑ concluded Chapter Two by recognizing the diverse set of questions philosophers ask. While the history of philosophy explains to a degree how these questions have come to be unified into one discipline, it does not explain why they *should* encompass a single, coherent domain. Let's try a different approach, focusing not on the subject matter of the questions themselves, but some shared characteristics of these subject matters. Although the questions of philosophy concern extremely diverse subject matters that have changed throughout history, they presently tend to focus on similar aspects within these subject matters. For example, metaphysicians don't ask whether or not CO_2 emissions cause global warming, they ask what causation is. Epistemologists don't seek knowledge of the planets, they seek knowledge of knowledge itself. Logicians are not concerned with particular arguments or inferences, but with the nature of inference. This shows that philosophers are concerned with reality at its most fundamental and general level. To be more precise, we can say that they appear to be focused on *the most fundamental and general concepts, principles, and features of the world, including our relationship to the world and to one another*. This characterization explains the diverse questions we find in philosophy and yields a coherent, distinguishing, and informative answer to the question of what philosophy is. Let's consider the various parts of this answer in light of what we've learned about philosophy in the preceding three chapters. We will then conclude this chapter by considering briefly some additional characteristics of philosophical inquiry.

Fundamental and General Concepts

A concept is an abstract mental grouping, and a reasonable, but not perfect, synonym of a concept is an *idea*. For example, suppose you visit an animal shelter and there you see several animals that bark, have fur, are domesticated, regulate their body heat by panting, and so forth. All these particulars fall under the concept of dog; the concept groups them together as one kind. Likewise, in another part of the shelter you find animals with fur, of small build, that purr and meow, and have claws. These animals fall under the concept of cat. In English we express the concept of dog with the word "dog," though French express the same concept with the word "chien," and Germans with the word "Hund." Concepts are not words, but we use words to express concepts. Further, concepts, as abstract mental groupings, may not correspond to anything in reality. Consider the concept of unicorn. Although unicorns do not exist, the concept of a unicorn exists: it is the concept of a horse-like animal with a horn coming out of its head and perhaps some magical powers.

Philosophers study the most fundamental and general concepts. What do we mean by saying that a concept is *fundamental?* We mean that other concepts, inquiries, and activities depend upon it; it is a foundation or basis for them. For example, the concept of knowledge is fundamental to our understanding of and interaction with the world because to understand the world *is* to have knowledge of it. Any attempts to understand the world—physics, geology, astronomy, chemistry, biology, psychology, sociology—all presuppose and build upon the concept of knowledge because they are all attempts to acquire knowledge.

Knowledge is fundamental in more ordinary ways because it underlies the everyday thinking, decisions, and activities of ordinary people. If I know that my favorite grocery store is closed, then I will do my shopping somewhere else. If I know that a particular movie is not one I will like, I may decide not to see it. If I am not aware of, I don't know of, a likely rainstorm, I may fail to bring my umbrella with me when I leave for work. Sometimes we even inquire explicitly about what we know. Perhaps I have two job offers, but I don't know which one will be the best choice.

I might even think: how do you know (i.e., decide) which career path is the best? We don't always use the term "knowledge" when we talk of our cognitive relationship to the world—we talk about deciding, being aware of, being certain, being sure about, believing—but the concept of knowing or understanding the world underlies this language and so is fundamental to our lives and behavior.

In contrast to the concept of knowledge, consider the concept of an automobile. This is not a fundamental concept. Our understanding of and interaction with the world and one another does not depend on it—for most of our history, there had not even been automobiles. If we didn't have the concept of an automobile, we could certainly get along in our ability to think about the world and others. This isn't the case with the concept of knowledge. We understand the world, and our interaction with the world, in terms of cognitively grasping (knowing) some things better than others. Consider the very ordinary experience of going shopping. I see next to the apples the price tag of 1 dollar per pound, and so I now know that they cost 1 dollar. I then look in my wallet and see only a 5 dollar bill, so I know I can buy up to 5 pounds of apples. Imaging trying to describe this situation without using the concept of knowledge or related concepts. It's impossible since every time we perceive the world and form beliefs about it, we are acquiring knowledge to some degree. None of this is to suggest that one must consciously think "There are apples in front of me" when looking at apples. We make use of fundamental concepts so regularly and so automatically that it is easy to forget how fundamental they are. The concept of knowledge, in contrast to the concept of an automobile, is therefore fundamental to our understanding of and interaction with the world and others.

What do we mean by a concept's being *general*? By *general* we understand *lacking in particularity*, and therefore having a *wide scope of application*. The concept of knowledge is general because it broadly applies across our experience. Philosophers are not concerned with knowledge about the oceans, or knowledge about the planets, or knowledge about early fetal development. These are particular areas of knowing, each corresponding to various disciplines. Philosophers are concerned with the general concept of knowledge: what is it merely to know.

While the subject matters of the subdisciplines of philosophy—as we considered in Chapter Two—are indeed diverse, the philosopher's concern in each of these subdisciplines is primarily focused on, among other things that we'll discuss, fundamental and general concepts. Even given our abbreviated discussion of these subdisciplines, it is not difficult to identify some of these fundamental and general concepts. Here's a brief list:

knowledge, justification (epistemology)

object, property, substance, causation (metaphysics)

inference, proof (logic)

right, wrong, good, bad, action (ethics)

meaning, reference, representation (philosophy of language)

belief, desire, mental causation (philosophy of mind)

Fundamental and General Principles

In addition to the concern with fundamental and general concepts, philosophy is concerned with fundamental and general principles. The best way to think of a principle is as a *rule* or *law*. Consider the following principle of logic:

Given the truth of: (1) If A then B
                      (2) A

It follows that: (3) B

This principle is called the principle of *Modus Ponens*. It is a principle of logical inference for which "A" and "B" represent statements. If you are presented with a belief that accords with this principle, then you should accept it. So suppose I say to you: "You really should have something to eat right now. You are about to start taking a long test, and if you are about to take a long test, then you should have something to eat beforehand." Should you accept my advice to have something to eat? If the conditions I stated are true: (1) you are about to take a test, and (2) if you are about to take a long test, then you should eat right before, then it follows, based on the principle of modus ponens, that you should have something to eat. This principle is general because it applies broadly: it doesn't matter what "A" and "B" are, the principle is still relevant. It is fundamental because these sorts of inferences are integral to our behavior, to our thinking, deliberating, making choices, decisions, and our ability to form an understanding of ourselves and the world. Such principles often influence us implicitly. Most people, if they see billows of smoke coming out of a home, will conclude that the house or something in the house is on fire. The reasoning is a simple application of modus ponens: (1) if there is smoke, then there is fire. (2) there is smoke; therefore, (3) there is fire. But most of us need not explicitly review, consciously consider, these steps before drawing the conclusion, though in fact these steps are exactly what justify our drawing the conclusion.

Let's consider another example. Ethical philosophers are concerned to show what the most basic principle of morality is, what rule or law underlies all our moral judgments. John Stuart Mill proposed the following principle: an action is morally right if it promotes more pleasure over pain (for all involved), and morally wrong if it promotes more pain over pleasure (for all involved) (*Utilitarianism* chapter 2). He called this the *Principle of Utility*. From this principle you can determine if a particular action is morally right or morally wrong. For example, suppose it is more of an inconvenience to me to take my used clothing to a charity thrift shop than to just throw it away. However, the benefit (or pleasure) of donating my used clothing, for those who will receive it, far outweighs my inconvenience. Therefore, according to the principle of utility, it is right of me to donate it, and wrong not to. Mill's principle is highly controversial in contrast to the principle of modus ponens, which is indisputably correct. Our point, however, is merely to show how philosophers are concerned with fundamental and general principles.

Both of these principles, the principle of utility and the principle of modus ponens, are fundamental and general. We are continually in the process of drawing inferences as we go about our day, explicitly and implicitly. It is one of the major ways in which we extend our knowledge. With regard to the principle of utility, a principle of ethical right and wrong, note that every action we perform has moral relevance, for moral principles are thought to deem, as permissible or not permissible, any action we may perform. To the extent that we think of morally wrong actions as actions that we should not do, then such a principle is fundamental to our lives. Once again, we typically do not explicitly consider and apply abstract ethical principles as we go about our day; rather, we are taught, through upbringing and learning, what actions are morally wrong and which are morally right. But what underlies these teachings? And what about controversial or difficult cases? Here is where these principles become explicitly relevant.

As a contrast, consider a principle that is neither general nor fundamental. A principle of good driving is that you should check your blind spot before changing lanes. This is surely an important principle of driving: the failure to check one's blind spot does in fact lead to accidents. But it is not a fundamental or general principle. It is not a principle that much builds upon, and it is very narrow in its scope of application.

Fundamental and General Features of the World

What about fundamental and general *features of the world?* Examples here will overlap with much of what we have said above. For example, while it will be conceded that moral right and moral wrong are fundamental and general concepts, it is an open question whether or not right and wrong are features of the world. Some philosophers argue that they are features of the world in the sense that they really exist. In the case of John Stuart Mill, mentioned above, he did think that right and wrong were features of the world, and empirically discernible features at that. Some have thought that right and wrong are mere concepts of the mind with nothing corresponding to them in reality; the concepts are akin to the concept of a unicorn: nothing in reality that falls under the concept. What is important to note is that philosophical inquiry is not merely conceptual inquiry, or it is at least a source of controversy when it is or is not.

In some cases philosophical inquiry does not appear to be merely conceptual. A philosopher's interest in the mind, and the components of the mind, does not appear to be merely conceptual. The mental is indeed a feature of our world, and philosophers strive to figure out what it is (is the mind just the brain, a distinct substance, something else?), and how it fits in with other things in the world. Likewise, philosophers' concern with language, with how language represents the world and expresses the thoughts of language users, is not merely a concern with the conceptual. Language is a part of the world, broadly conceived. So the concern to understand language is a concern with a feature of the world.

The World, Our Relationship to It and to One Another

The answer we are developing in this chapter is that philosophy is an intellectual discipline concerned with the most fundamental and general concepts, principles, and features of the world, our relationship to it and to one another. Let's discuss briefly this last component of the answer: the world, our relationship to it and to one another. We understand "the world" in the broadest sense imaginable (not merely in the sense of the physical world). Most disciplines are narrower in their focus. The biologist is generally concerned with living entities. The geologist is concerned with the formation in the Earth, its components, methods of retrieval, and so forth. Philosophers narrow their interest as well, but only in the sense that they are concerned with the most fundamental and general features of reality. They are not otherwise concerned with any particular part of reality.

Further, it is clear that much of a philosopher's concern is with our relationship to the world, with how we interact with the world. Epistemology and its concern with knowledge is a good example of this. We interact with the world, in part, by having knowledge *about* the world. So the study of knowledge is not so much the study of something in the world but the study of how we relate to the world. Likewise, consider an ethicists' concern with action. We interact with the world through action. Philosophers are not concerned with interaction such as building roads or planting crops—these are very particular cases of action. Rather, philosophers are concerned with the structure or form of action in general, what characterizes and distinguishes action from cases of mere bodily movement, voluntary action as opposed to coerced action.

Finally, philosophers are concerned with our relationship to one another. Since other people are a part of the world, broadly conceived, we could have perhaps left this out. But given the prominence of ethics in philosophy, it is worth the emphasis. We consider ourselves to have obligations toward one another, and the nature of such obligations is the study of ethics. Political philosophy can also be thought of as concerned with our relationship to one another. To the extent that politics concerns organizing a community and political philosophers are interested in the justification or warrant for community authority, then it too concerns our relationships with one another at a very fundamental and general level. Philosophers are not, in contrast, concerned with studying particular governments, policies, leaders, or elections; these involve particular instances of our relationships with one another.

Qualification and the History of Philosophy

I have argued in this chapter for the characterization of philosophy as follows: *philosophy is an intellectual discipline concerned with the most fundamental and general concepts, principles, and features of the world, our relationship to it and to one another.* This characterization accounts for the diverse questions and topics that we find presently unified in the discipline of philosophy. That said, any characterization of philosophy is bound to be controversial to some degree and certainly will be open to argument as to its correctness. My purpose has been to give those who are relatively new to philosophy some working understanding of philosophy as a whole. As you read more philosophy and gain further exposure to its topics and questions, you can better understand and apply this characterization of philosophy and understand the ways that it may need to be qualified.

With that in mind, we should consider one way in which this characterization does fall short and explain why any characterization of philosophy will ultimately fall short of perfection. This characterization falls short given that some of the topics of the various subdisciplines of philosophy do not seem to be "general" and "fundamental." For example, some ethical philosophy concerns what is called *applied ethics*, an ethical concern with particular cases of right and wrong. For example, a prominent discussion in recent years has been that of the morality of abortion.[1] But neither the practice nor the concept of abortion are fundamental and general. Abortion is a very particular kind of action, and yet ethical philosophers have debated extensively whether or not it is morally wrong or morally permissible. So here is a part of philosophy that does not fit well into the characterization I have given.

One might think: but *right* and *wrong* are general and fundamental concepts, so the discussion of abortion does fit into our characterization of philosophy since we are concerned with the rightness or wrongness of abortion. The problem with this response is evident in the following

---

1 Two classical works by philosophers on this subject are Judith Thomson's "A Defense of Abortion" and Thomas Marquis'"Why Abortion Is Immoral."

obviously false claim: since metaphysics is concerned with causation, then a medical researcher's attempt to show that smoking causes lung cancer is really an instance of doing philosophy (and metaphysics for that matter). This is absurd, of course. In fact, in the case of causation, philosophers are concerned with causation in general, not with particular applications of it. But in the case of some ethical discussions, in contrast, philosophers are concerned with particular applications of the concepts of right and wrong.

Let's consider another example. Philosophy of religion concerns, among other things, the nature and existence of God. But God, whether you believe in his existence or not, is not a fundamental or general concept or feature of the world. This is not to say that God, depending on one's religious beliefs, is not important. Something may be critically important and yet not be fundamental or general. And yet the history of philosophy has discussed, and continues to discuss, proofs both for and against the existence of God. This constitutes another counter-example to the characterization of philosophy that we have developed in this chapter.

In response to these counter-examples, two points are in order. First, while these sorts of counter-examples exist, they are not significantly numerous. In addition, these counter-examples often have a very close relationship with philosophical discussions of the fundamental and general. For example, a fire investigator can determine the cause of a housefire without any special, philosophical knowledge of causation. But determining the morality of difficult moral dilemmas, such as abortion, ultimately requires a deeper understanding of morality, the kind that falls under our characterization of philosophy. Second, and more important, it is likely that any meaningful characterization of philosophy will leave out some things that are in fact a part of philosophy. This results from this historical nature of philosophy. Philosophy is a historical discipline—as we reviewed in Chapter Two—that has evolved over the course of its history. There is no one person or persons who are "in charge" of what stays in philosophy and what does not. So while most of philosophy may be correctly characterized by the answer we have considered in this chapter, it should not be a surprise that some aspects of philosophy are not well represented by it. Further, philosophy (as with other intellectual disciplines) is a human endeavor. While intellectual inquiries tend to be grouped according to similarity of subject matter, in fact no one can forbid what can or cannot be studied. Some topics or questions may have an enduring legacy in philosophy simply because of the fact that those who do philosophy are interested in them or consider the answers to such questions to be relevant to other philosophical topics.

In light of this, we can amend our characterization of philosophy as follows: philosophy is an intellectual discipline concerned with the most fundamental and general concepts, principles, and features of the world and our interaction with the world and one another. Because philosophy is a historical discipline—it started out as roughly the search for knowledge in all areas and has evolved and narrowed over time—some of the parts of philosophy do not necessarily fit well into this characterization.

Other Characteristics of Philosophy

Before concluding, it is worth noting some other characteristics of philosophy that can be discerned from our discussion of the parts and history of philosophy in chapters Two and Three. These are characteristics that you will recognize if you continue to study philosophy, its topics, and its figures. First, philosophy tends to involve the nonempirical study of phenomena where a nonempirical approach is appropriate. "Empirical" means having to do with observation, with sensory experience, and so "nonempirical" inquiry does not involve a dependency on sensory experience. In contrast, we talk of the empirical sciences (such as chemistry, physics, biology). As we can see from the discussion of the questions of philosophy, as presently practiced, philosophy tends toward nonempirical inquiry. Questions about the nature of inferential relations, for example, simply do not appear to be questions that can be answered empirically. But I note that it is not necessarily a philosopher's intent to pursue truth nonempirically; it merely happens to be the case that the questions of philosophy are not amenable to empirical investigation.

Second, philosophy concerns understanding in general our capabilities and limitations as rational creatures. This is especially apparent in much of ancient and modern philosophy. Rationality, our thinking capability, is one of the things that distinguishes humans from other creatures. From this arises the question of what constitutes our being rational, what are the correct principles of rational thought and rational action. For example, being capable of knowledge appears to be one thing that characterizes rational creatures. Further, rational creatures are capable of drawing inferences. For many philosophers, the concern to understand our rational capabilities is implicit in their philosophizing; for others such as Immanuel Kant, David Hume, and Rene Descartes, the concern is explicit and prominent.

Finally, philosophy is concerned to understand the progress, limits, and possibility of the sciences. Science denotes a systematic approach to knowledge in a subject matter, and to the extent that a subject matter is a science, it constitutes a major intellectual achievement. The concern with science is not merely evident by the subdiscipline of philosophy called "philosophy of science." A good deal of metaphysics and epistemology, as one looks through the history of philosophy, was motivated by a concern for the sciences. In many ways, but not always, the philosopher's perspective toward science was one of support: philosophers were concerned to give legitimacy to the progress of the sciences, to show that the sciences were sources of genuine understanding and knowledge about the world. As you read more philosophy, you will see this theme repeatedly appearing.

Conclusion

As an intellectual discipline, the value of philosophy is found in the knowledge it produces. Sometimes this value is difficult to see in comparison with other kinds of disciplines. The value of engineering, for example, seems obvious: it produces products that benefit the well-being of humans. But the knowledge that philosophy imparts, while not perhaps producing products, has the potential to change those who study it. And in this lies its value. This may be obvious in some areas of philosophy: a better understanding of ethical concepts surely will benefit one who contemplates many of the important questions of our society. But even as we grapple with other questions—questions of knowledge, existence, language—we gain a better grasp of who we are as rational creatures, and how we understand, or don't understand, the world around us.

In addition, as the great Twentieth-century philosopher Bertrand Russell stated, "philosophy has a value—perhaps its chief value—through the greatness of the objects which it contemplates" (*The Problems of Philosophy* 114). Part of this greatness lies in the extreme diversity we find in these objects of contemplation. Our task has been to work together toward a meaningful and useful characterization of what unifies these diverse topics. This unified understanding can serve as a source of clarity and structure to help you better understand and approach the great questions and topics of philosophical inquiry.